Reycraft Books
145 Huguenot Street
New Rochelle, NY 10801

reycraftbooks.com

Reycraft Books is a trade imprint and trademark of Newmark Learning LLC.

Text © Kaitlin Sikes

All rights reserved. No portion of this book may be reproduced, stored in a retrieval system, or transmitted in any form or by any means, electronic, mechanical, photocopying, recording, or otherwise, without written permission from the publisher. For information regarding permission, please contact info@reycraftbooks.com.

Educators and Librarians: Our books may be purchased in bulk for promotional, educational, or business use. Please contact sales@reycraftbooks.com.

This is a work of fiction. Names, characters, places, dialogue, and incidents described either are the product of the author's imagination or are used fictitiously. Any resemblance to actual persons, living or dead, is entirely coincidental.

Sale of this book without a front cover or jacket may be unauthorized. If this book is coverless, it may have been reported to the publisher as "unsold or destroyed" and may have deprived the author and publisher of payment.

Library of Congress Control Number: 2024948192

Hardcover ISBN: 978-1-4788-8538-2
Paperback ISBN: 978-1-4788-8539-9

Author photo: Courtesy of Kristin Grover Images
Illustrator photo: Courtesy of Mel Cerri

Printed in Dongguan, China. 8557/1124/21851
10 9 8 7 6 5 4 3 2 1

First Edition published by Reycraft Books 2025.

Reycraft Books and Newmark Learning LLC, support diversity, the First Amendment and celebrate the right to read.

written by **Kaitlin Sikes**
illustrated by **Mel Cerri**

Gray clouds gather.

One drop of water waits.

Thunder rumbles.

One drop
sinks...
through sandy soil,
cradled by the aquifer.

One drop flows
    along an underground stream and bubbles...
        up past caves,
            through a vent,
                into a cool spring.

One drop
shimmers
in a marsh dance,
glides along a restless tributary.

One drop
skims
a snapping lake...

One drop
   leaves land
      and sweeps out to the Atlantic Ocean.

As day tumbles into night,
it surfs the warm Gulf Stream.

One drop
flows north
passing an iceberg.

Whoosh!

A whale's tail
 whips one drop into a strait.

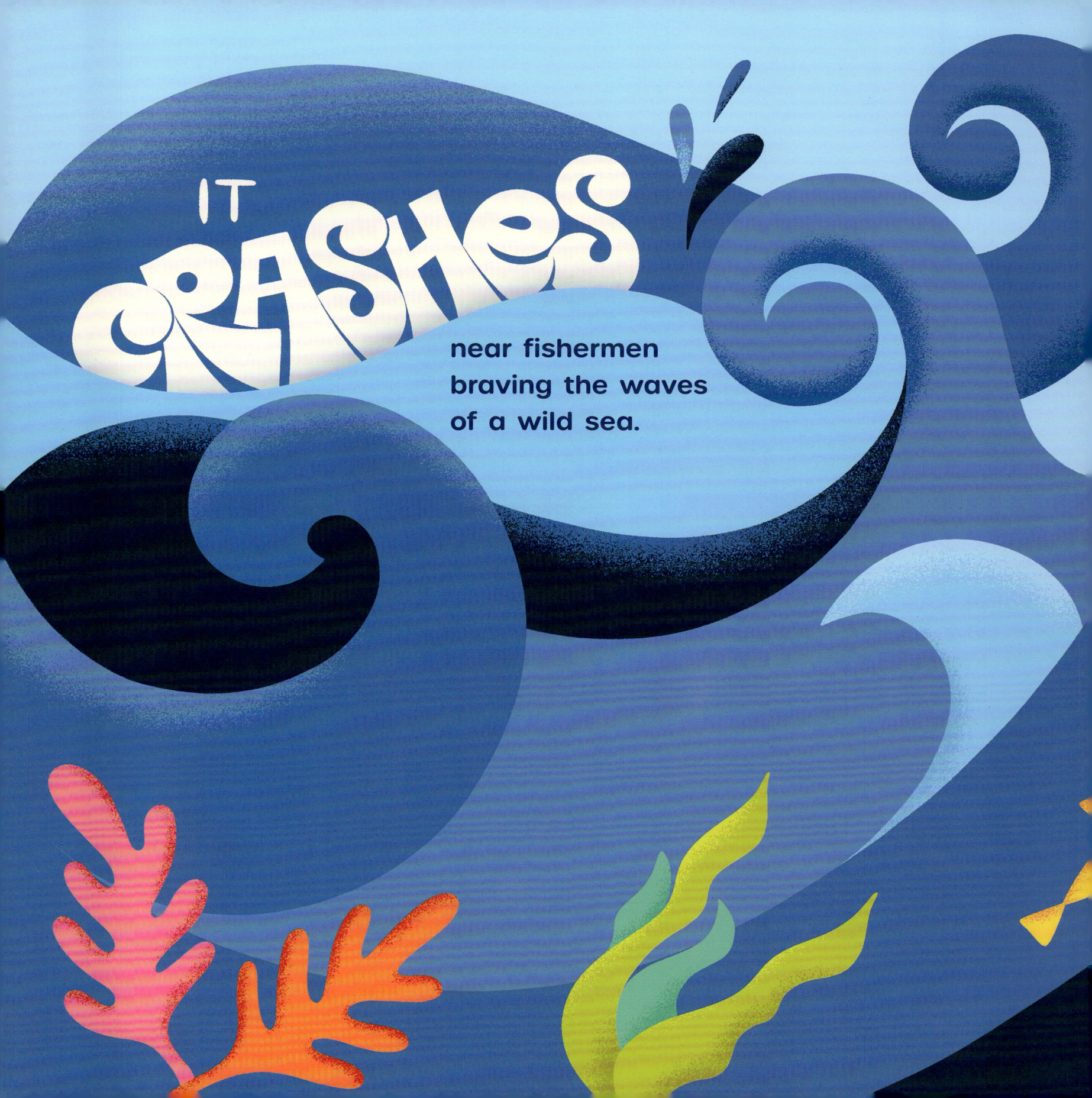

...is scooped up in a little bucket,
poured into a mud castle moat,
catching a ride on a yellow boot.

An **AQUIFER** is an underground layer of rock that contains water. The Floridan aquifer sits beneath much of the southeastern United States. The aquifer is deep within the earth and usually has a "lid" on it (like a pot of water). In some places the "lid" is thicker and yet in others, the water comes right up to the surface of the earth through a spring vent resulting in "springs". There are more than 800 freshwater springs in Florida—more than anywhere else on earth! The springs in Florida are mostly cold but did you know there are also hot springs in the world?

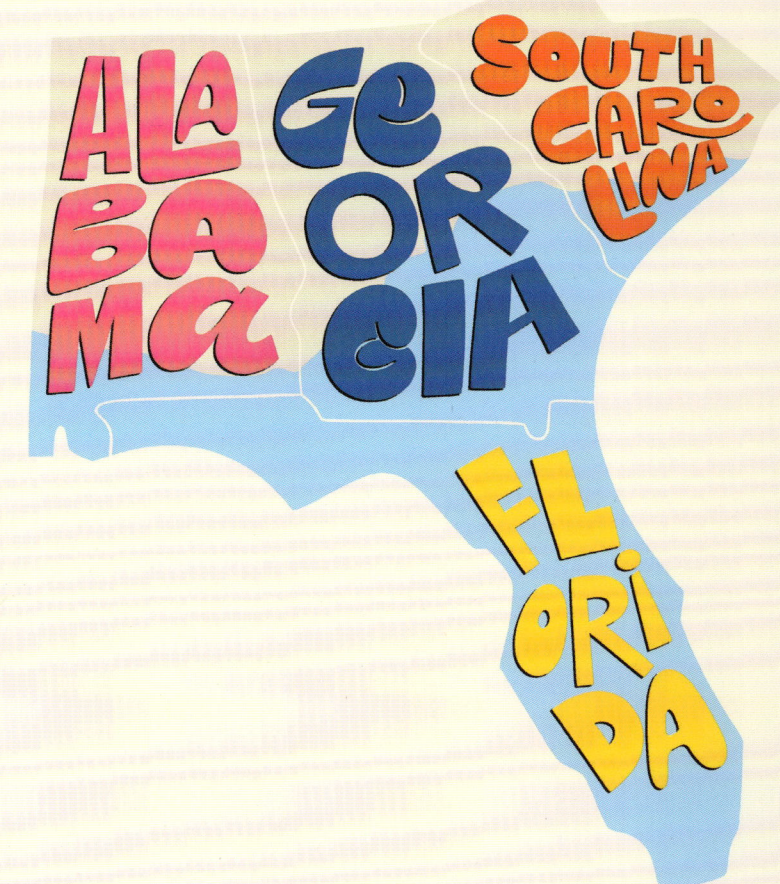

A **MARSH** is where the land is often covered by water and there aren't many trees. Marshes can be freshwater, saltwater, or brackish (a mixture of the two). Marshes can be tidal (they change with the tide) or non-tidal. Did you know that the largest freshwater marsh in the United States is the Florida Everglades?

The drop of water flows out of the marsh and follows water pathways that gradually get bigger.

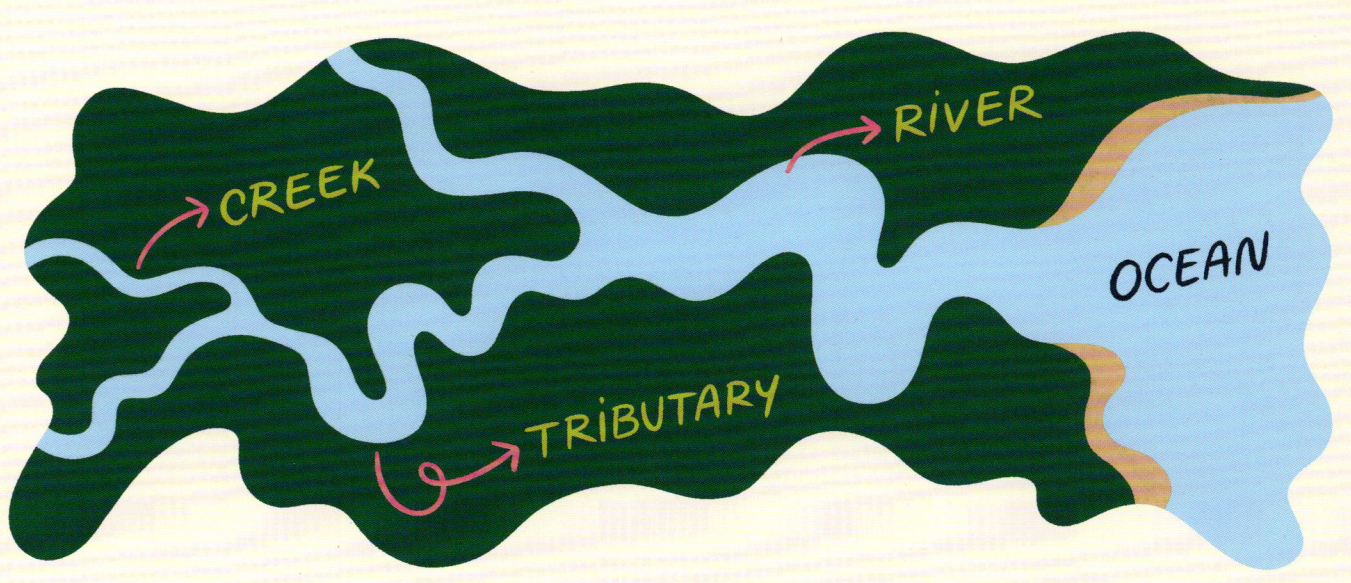

It then meets up with the **GULF STREAM**, which starts in the Gulf of Mexico and runs north, along the Atlantic coast of the United States. Did you know that the Gulf Stream brings warm water from the tropics to the North Atlantic and helps warm the weather in Europe?

An **ICEBERG** is a large floating mass of ice that has detached from a glacier and floated out to sea. Did you know that icebergs make lots of noises? They groan if they break or if they scrape another iceberg.

A **WATERFALL** forms when water falls from a height, usually when water falls over a cliff. But did you know that the tallest waterfall on earth is underwater? It is called the Denmark Strait cataract and it is three times longer than any waterfall on land, with water plunging from the Greenland Sea into the Irminger Sea.

An **ESTUARY** is always found along a coast and it is where river and sea water mix. This in-between zone is teeming with life. What other in-between zones can you think of?

Glossary

A **STRAIT** is a narrow passage of water connecting two large areas of water.

A **SEA** is a large body of salt water that is surrounded in part (or whole) by land.

A **BAY** is a body of water connected to an ocean or lake, formed by an indentation of the shoreline.

KAITLIN SIKES

lives in Northeast Florida, near the Saint Johns River. This unusual river that flows north made her wonder... with no nearby mountains, where did it come from? And where was it going? The answers revealed unexpected global connections. Kaitlin is passionate about writing books that inspire wonder and loves searching for those stories alongside her husband and two children. When she isn't writing or exploring the natural world, she works as a Pediatric Nurse Practitioner. One day, she would love to visit the beautiful places featured in this book.

MEL CERRI

is a Brazilian-born lettering artist and illustrator, who brings her vibrant energy to life through captivating images. With over a decade of experience, her work boasts a bold style brimming with color, inspired by her Latin heritage and her love for all things playful. Mel's work has illustrated campaigns for global brands like Nike, Apple, Disney, and Facebook. While initially drawn to advertising, Mel's freelance journey as a graphic designer led to a thriving career in illustration, where the vibrant signature of her work results in expressive graphics, murals, branding, and more.